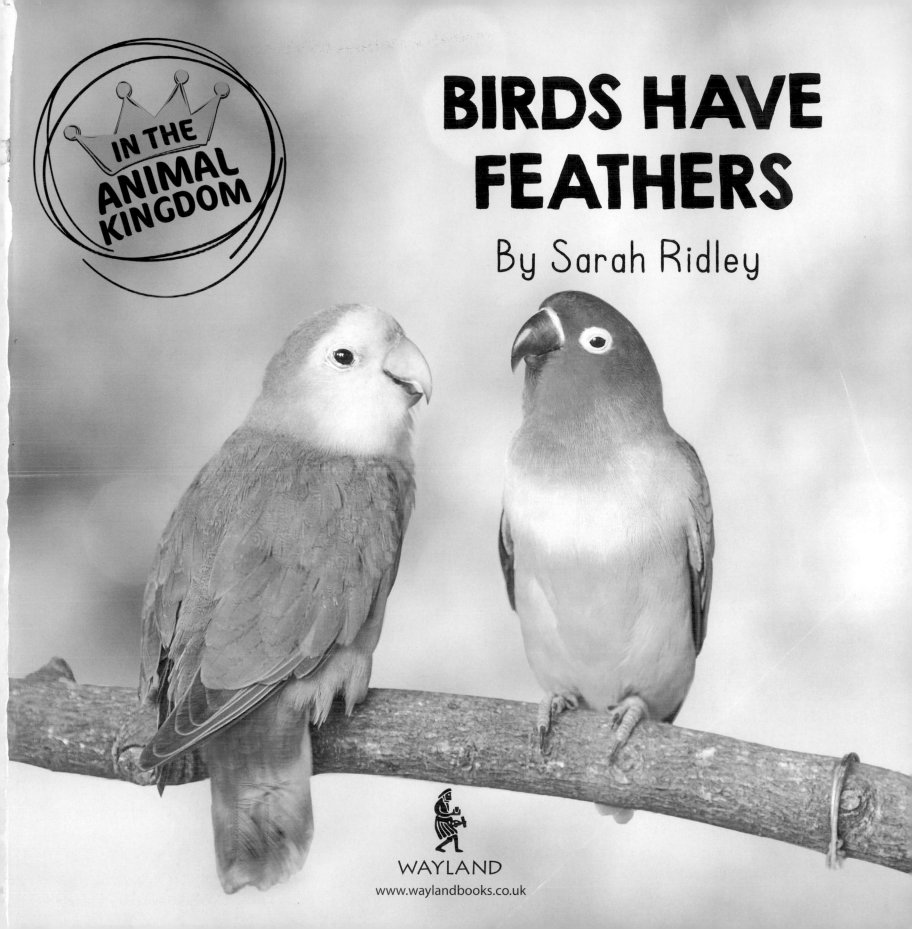

BIRDS HAVE FEATHERS

By Sarah Ridley

IN THE ANIMAL KINGDOM

WAYLAND
www.waylandbooks.co.uk

First published in Great Britain in 2018
by Wayland

Copyright © Hodder and Stoughton,
2018

Editor: Sarah Peutrill
Designer: Lisa Peacock

ISBN: 978 1 5263 0928 0

Printed and bound in China

Wayland, an imprint of
Hachette Children's Group
Part of Hodder and Stoughton
Carmelite House
50 Victoria Embankment
London EC4Y 0DZ
An Hachette UK Company
www.hachette.co.uk
www.hachettechildrens.co.uk

Every attempt has been made to
clear copyright. Should there be any
inadvertent omission please apply to the
publisher for rectification.

MIX
Paper from
responsible sources
FSC® C104740

Picture credits: aabeele/Shutterstock: 7t. Jeffrey B Banke/Shutterstock: 7b.
BMJ/Shutterstock: 2b, 9b. Bobbushphoto/iStockphoto: 2t, 15t. Maurizio
Bobora/iStockphoto: 20. Butterfly Hunter/Shutterstock: front cover. John
Carnemolla/Shutterstock: 13t. ChameleonsEye/iStockphoto: 23t. Chrispo/
Shutterstock: 9t. Johan Dalstrom/Shutterstock: 11t. Dietlinde B DuPlessis/
Shutterstock: 22t. FRDMR/Shutterstock: 3t, 17t. Peter Fulzia/Shutterstock:
9b. Gallinego Media/Shutterstock: 10, 11b. Ana Gram/Shutterstock:
17b. Dennis Jacobsen/Shutterstock: 23c. Kathy Kay/Shutterstock: 15c.
Andrzej Kubik/Shutterstock: 12. William Leaman/Alamy: 16b. Ole Jorgen
Liodden/Nature PL: 13b. David Litman/Shutterstock: 14. Francesco de
Marco/Shutterstock: 21t. Rolf Nussbaumer/Nature PL:15r. Fred Olivier/
Nature PL: 19t. PJ Photography/Shutterstock: 3b, 17c. Andy Rouse/
Nature PL: 21b. rugco/Shutterstock: 8t. Fedor Selvanov/Shutterstock: 22b.
vladsilver/Shutterstock: 23b. StevenRussellSmithPhotos/Shutterstock: 6b.
tathoms/Shutterstock: 6t. apichon tee/Shutterstock: 1. Vasily Vishnevskiy/
Shutterstock: 18. Abi Warner/Shutterstock: 19b.

CONTENTS

The animal kingdom

Scientists sort all living things on Earth into five huge groups called kingdoms. All animals belong in the animal kingdom.

The animal kingdom is divided into two very large groups. The invertebrates are animals without a backbone and the vertebrates are animals with a backbone.

INVERTEBRATES

ANIMAL KINGDOM

Then we divide the vertebrates up again, into five large groups: fish, amphibians, reptiles, birds and mammals.

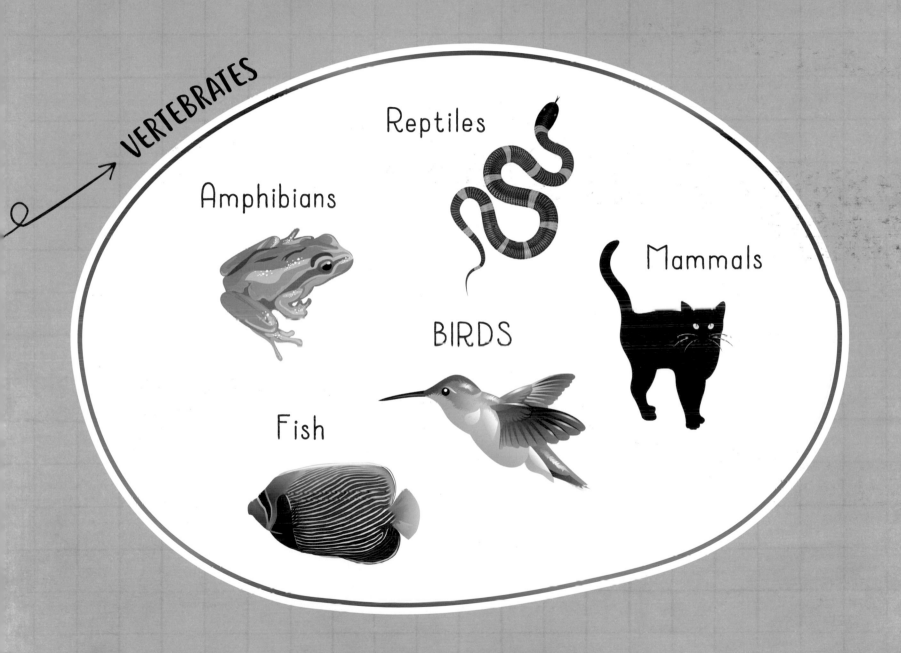

VERTEBRATES

Reptiles

Amphibians

Mammals

BIRDS

Fish

Read on to find out what makes an animal a bird.

All birds have feathers

Light, strong feathers grow from birds' skin and help them to fly.

Roseate spoonbill

Northern cardinal

Fluffy, downy feathers help to keep birds warm.

Mallard

Turkey

Feathers zip together to keep out the wind, water or rain.

Some male birds display their feathers to show off to females.

The ancestors of birds were small dinosaurs with feathers.

Birds have two legs and two wings

Flamingoes walk through water on their long legs.

The greenfinch flies from tree to tree, using its feet and toes to cling to branches.

Webbed feet help ducks swim across water.

Wide wings and huge
talons help sea eagles
catch and carry food.

Birds, like mammals,
can turn the food they
eat into heat – they are
warm-blooded.

Most birds can fly

Everything about birds helps them to fly.

Feathers and beaks are light.

Wings flap up and down.

Hollow bones are very light and full of air.

Legs tuck up under the body.

This bird is a swallow. It spends most of its day flying, catching and eating insects in the air.

Swans are heavy
birds so they
need huge wings
to hold them up.

Male skylarks fly
high into the sky,
singing to attract
a mate.

What other animals
can fly?

Some birds cannot fly

Ostriches are the biggest birds in the world.
They cannot fly but they can run very fast.

The kiwi lives on the ground, where it finds worms, insects and seeds to eat.

Penguins have wings that have become flippers for swimming fast.

Birds breathe air, like us. When penguins dive underwater, they hold their breath.

Birds have a beak or a bill

The shape of the bird's beak or bill matches the food it eats.

Marbled godwits use their long bill to grab worms and shrimps that live in mud.

Birds have no teeth so they cannot chew their food.

The bee-eater catches insects with its thin, pointed beak.

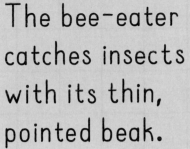

Hummingbirds have long thin beaks to reach the nectar inside flowers.

This pelican has caught a fish in its stretchy bill.

Most birds build nests

Nests are a place where birds can keep their eggs safe and care for their young.

Female ruby-throated hummingbird with her chicks

The male weaver bird uses grass to weave a hanging nest.

Weaver bird

Puffins nest in burrows on cliffs.

Puffin

A pair of storks build their huge nest of twigs, grass and leaves.

Stork

All birds lay eggs

Marsh warbler

After mating, the female bird grows an egg inside her body.

Some types of bird lay one egg, while others lay many. Eggs need to be kept warm or the chicks growing inside will die.

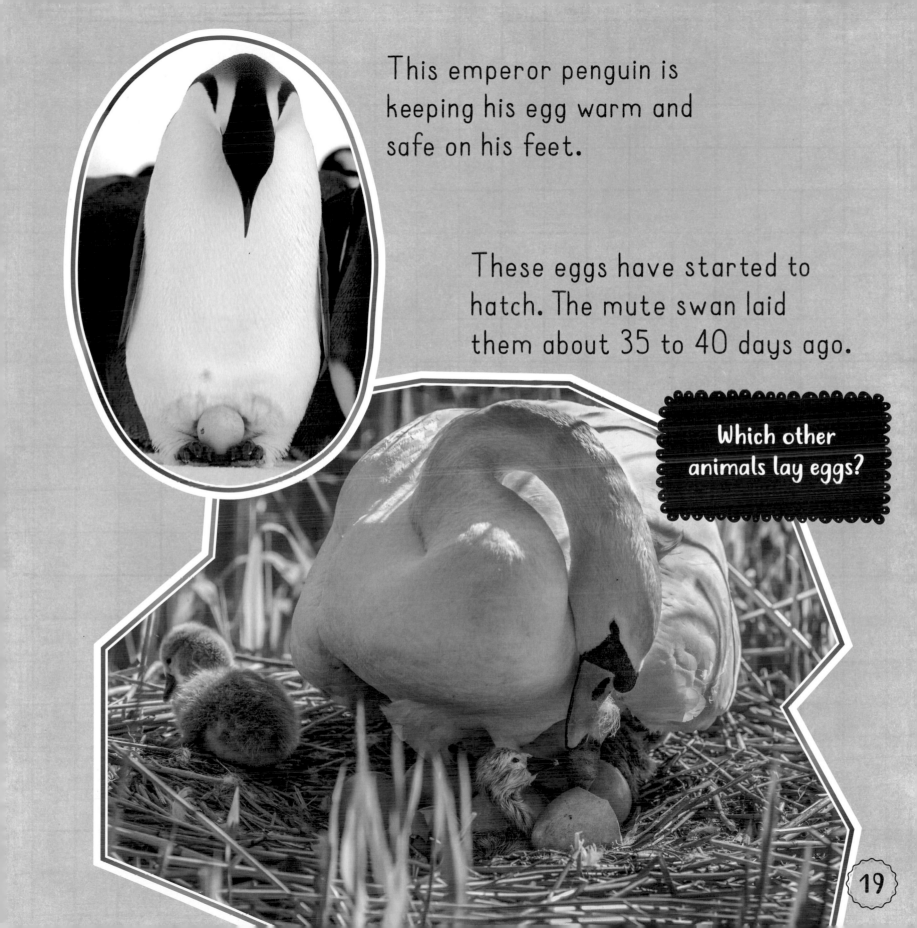

This emperor penguin is keeping his egg warm and safe on his feet.

These eggs have started to hatch. The mute swan laid them about 35 to 40 days ago.

Which other animals lay eggs?

19

Birds take care of their young

Reed warbler parents bring food to
their chicks while they grow feathers
and become strong.

Cuckoos trick other birds into bringing up their young. This redstart is feeding a cuckoo chick as if it were her own.

The black-browed albatross has one chick each year. The parents spend most of their time out at sea finding fish to feed it.

Birds live all over the world

Gila woodpeckers nest in cacti in Mexico and the USA.

Toucans live in the rainforests of South America.

The superb fairy wren lives in gardens and woodlands in Australia.

Many birds migrate, like these barnacle geese. They live in Greenland and Norway over the summer, and fly to Scotland for the winter, where it is warmer.

Gentoo penguins live in Antarctica.

There are over 10,000 different species, or kinds, of bird!

Which birds named in this book cannot fly?

Answer: Turn to pages 12–13.

Glossary

amphibian An animal that can live both on land and in water.

ancestor An animal that lived in the past and from which a living animal has developed.

backbone A row of small bones that are connected together to form the spine.

hatch To come out of an egg.

insect An animal with six legs and a body divided into three parts.

invertebrate An animal without a backbone.

mate A male or female partner for an animal.

migrate To move from one place to another, according to the season.

nectar A sweet liquid that is made inside flowers.

species A kind of living thing, such as a mallard or emperor penguin.

talon A long curved claw.

warm-blooded Animals that can keep their bodies at the same temperature even when it is cold by changing the food they eat into heat and energy.

young Another word for animal babies.

Index